EXTRAORDINARY WAYS TO RAISE YOUR PARENTING EQ

BEING PARENT - PREMIER EDITION

BHUSHAN KHAIRNAR

ISBN 979-888530610-2

To my sons, Aditya & Sviten

Contents

Preface

Finland is the Happiest Country in the World and Japan has the third highest ranking in Quality of Life. Both the countries are ranked highest in Parenting EQ.

USA : 90 - 104

UK : 85 - 99

Canada : 85 - 99

Asia : 80 - 94

India: 75 - 89

Japan : 130 - 144

Finland : 135 - 149

Parenting styles are personal and often depend on our own unique situation, but there is much we can learn from how Finnish and Japanese parenting styles.

The brunch book,"Extraordinary Ways to Raise your Parenting EQ" is useful to the parents of one year to the mature teenager. The book shall guide you to raise independent, healthy, happy, courageous children. So that you shall enjoy the intellectual, emotional and spiritual journey of being parent.

What makes Parenting at Japan and Finland better than the rest of the World? Let's check the areas of children life, they are focusing on:

Experiencing the World

In Japan, at very young age, children go to school unaccompanied, even if it means taking a city bus or train and traversing busy streets. The chapter has been designed to answer your queries, doubts and perception about the experiencing the world and your role as parent.

How your children understand the world around them? What are the experiences the parents should plan for? What experiences shape the successful and happy life of your children?

The world that your children see in the map, watch on YouTube and read in magazines and article is not enough to generate deep experience that can help them to succeed in the real world. Trip to real jungle or even at zoo is far significant and memorable experience than to study in class. Ultimately, your children are going to live in this real world. Experiences will shape their behaviour and attitude towards the world.

Health - Food and Activities

The chapter is about the food and food habits of your children. The most important thing is to teach your kid about food is that food isn't just about taste.The primary purpose of food is not just to give you some sort of a euphoric sensual experience three times a day. That's a nice bonus but it's not the primary purpose of food.

The primary purpose of food is to fuel your body. Just to give your body the proper balance of nutritional components that it needs to function at an optimal level. If you get that into a kid's head early on, that's going to put them on the right path for life.

Every individual has different metabolism, hence, your children too. How to choose the right food and develop food habit in your children?

Teach them about Money

In this chapter, You shall know how to teach children about money, becoming financially responsible and the core of creating wealth.

Do you want to teach our kids about money? What it is where it comes from. How wealth is created and what it can do for you. And the people around you and school doesn't even try to address this issue. We spend 20-24 years learning science, maths, arts and many more subjects and then we get degrees. Then we spend the rest of our lives trying to make money. We're going to look at this craziness, when we dive into career and finances.

Think, we don't teach our kids about the creation of wealth, no one will. You can be sure of that we want to implant the fundamentals firmly in their brains so that they'll have the opportunity to be financially successful and have abundance in their lives we want to teach our children about.

Set Safe and Secure Environment (Physical and Psychological)

The chapter is about how to create the safe and secure environment around your children and how to make them independent children.

Our primary role as parents is to make sure that our children possess the competence to cope with the challenges of life when we're not there to guide them. So we've got to help them become self-sufficient. We've got to equip them with the skills and the tools, they need to navigate their own life in the way they see fit to develop a sense of efficacy and to learn to trust themselves to make good decisions for their own lives.

Their physical safety is first and foremost keeping them from getting hurt, keeping them out of danger, making sure they have proper food, clothing and shelter. Then comes psychological safety. Children need the experience of living in a rational universe a world in which facts are treated as facts, truth is respected, question asking is valued and not punished. An environment in which a child's desire to understand is honored and nurtured.

Career - How to choose and grow

The chapter is about - How to prepare your children for fulfilling and happy career? What we can do as a parent? Who decides the career - children or parent? And other few important questions.

Parents are worried most about their children's fulfilling career. It decides children's financial safety, their well-being and about their happiness. The process to prepare children for the challenges and opportunities is simple but not easy.

Quality way of Thinking

The chapter is about How children observe, analyse and interpret the world. It's about the process of thinking and how parents can help children build healthy, valuable and quality way to think.

The quality of your children's lives will be based to a huge extent on their ability to think in a high quality way. Parents should teach how to think while schools teaches what to think. Kids are taught next to nothing about reason, rationality and the importance of critical thinking in the schools. Can you imagine school teaching kids how to think critically, how to question everything.

Parents should teach how to think while schools teaches what to think. Kids are taught the lowest level of thinking in school - how to regurgitate information.

Self-Expression

The chapter is about creating proper environment, designing activities and proper care which encourage children to express freely and develop responsibility as they grow mature. It shall teach parents about the various ways to ensure the growth of creative expression in your children.

Self-Expression is about everything you do and say. Self-Expression means all the opportunities that you have to express yourself from the clothes you put on, in the morning to the share posts on social media, to share your success stories with your friends at night.

Self-expression is crucial for the development of a child's identity, self-confidence and sense of belonging to the world.

Managing Emotional and Rational Life

In this chapter, parents shall learn about children emotional and rational life and how to manage and utilise the emotions and use intellectual capacities to make their life better.

Parents can teach their children to choose and teach them to become author of their life. Healthy emotional life is indispensable for living a happy successful life and our intellectual abilities is our basic tool of survival. Whether it's emotions or rational thinking, as a human being we have right to choose.

Setting Goals and Achieving them

The chapter is about how to develop the habits of setting goals and achieving them and how to stay focused during the process. The goal may be day to day, life long, short term or long term.

To be successful human being, setting goals and achieve them is an important part of our routine life. Schools and many parents fails to teach this important skill of how to teach your children to set goals consciously and stay focused to achieve them. Here is an opportunity to make it happen in your children's life.

Managing Digital Life

The chapter is about how to prepare your children to collaboratively live in the digital world and physical world to widen the scope of better life.

Many experts and analysts are unable to see through the real issue and addressing only half reality about the digital world. They see the digital world as positive and negative only.

The digital world is only replica of our physical world. It has provided larger space for Human Imagination, so, we find many new and uncomfortable life over there. This is the reason why children gets fast addicted to the digital media. Their imaginations are far more free than ours. In the process of growth, somehow we have lost the capacity to imagine the world with own free eyes but fortunately children haven't.

Social Life

The chapter will give a comprehensive view of social life and how to ensure the better present and future social life of their children.

The quality of life is determined by what kind of people we are surrounded with. The same is applicable to your children's life. Teach them to become conscious decision maker in choosing friends and people with whom they desire to spend more time, exchange values and express themselves.

Implementing Parenting Goals

Action is the key to achieving your goals. Whatever situation, stage and economic condition, you are, start implementing them in the Being Parents ways.

You shall know the effective ways to implement the knowledge that you have gained in above 11 chapters.

Acknowledgements

I express thanks to my both children, Aditya (14 Yr) - Entrepreneur, the Youngest Author of India and who has a Registered Patent in his name and Sviten (7 Yr) for making our life joyous and for wonderful parenting experiences. I am thankful to my Parents, Lt. Shri Ashok Khairnar and Shree Ratna Khairnar for instilling the broad life vision.

My completion of this book could not have been possible without the support of my robot researcher and decision intelligence, Noam Polyglot. Noam is a Robot with artificial intelligence capacities who has been helping me in surfing and getting research done in unbelievable time and accuracy. Noam has helped me analyse and organise parent and children growth data which helped me to find out the realistic parenting growth parameters.

I also thank to Ms. Sonali Kapure Parmar for making me add the chapter of safety and security.

I especially thanks to the Block-Chain technology innovators and people who have contributed to its growth. Without which the secure and advance systems of Brunch Books (International Blockchain based Book Registry System) would not have been possible.

Finally, to my caring, loving, and supportive wife, Khushbu: my deepest gratitude. Your encouragement when the times got rough are much appreciated and duly noted. It was a great comfort and relief to know that you were willing to provide travelling support through your company, Tourinfowale.online and management of our household activities while I completed my work. My heartfelt thanks.

Prologue

WHAT'S BEING PARENT?

Parenting is an intellectual, emotional and spiritual journey that simply can't be duplicated in any other way or even just being around children can be one of the best things about life. If you're a parent you probably know how much pure joy and happiness and laughter children can bring. On the other hand parenting has been called one of the hardest and most thankless jobs in the world. Raising children can involve incredibly difficult and sometimes painful circumstances - divorce happens, custody battles happen. You may have a child with health problems or with special needs You might be at the end of your hope simply just trying to hang on, while raising a teenager.

Being a parent is an awesome responsibility. The life of another human being is in your hands. When the process begins, they're totally dependent on you. They can't walk, they can't talk, they can't hold their heads up. If you left them alone for hours, they wouldn't survive. As they get older, they look to you for everything important their food their shelter their clothing as they develop they look to you for values, for morals, for a sense of life.

You're under a microscope - everything you say, everything you do, you are what human being means to them. Your level of health is what health means, they look at your marriage as an example of what marriage means, your career is what career means as a parent. So what is being a parent is all about what is your approach and belief towards life.

People think that parenting is about never saying no to our kids you know treating like these fragile little statues a in a closet and putting bubble wrap them and and only feeding them they want it's not about that. It's about negotiating, it's about a tuning, it's engaging, and it's about connecting with our children. But the problem of being parent is that the parents want the easy way. When parents don't understand - what is being parent, the parenting become painful and hard job.

It's up to us to define what they need to know and to teach it to them to be successful humans because it's just not going to happen in schools, colleges nor the government is going to teach them. We have got to teach our children what they need to know to navigate through life. I believe that our job as parents is to raise independent, healthy, happy and courageous children. Parenting entails these 11 things in order to raise children:

- Experiencing the World
- Health - Food and Activities
- Teach them about Money
- Set Safe and Secure Environment (Physical and Psychological)
- Career - How to choose and grow
- Quality way of Thinking
- Self-Expression
- Managing Emotional and Rational Life
- Setting Goals and Achieving them
- Managing Digital Life
- Social Life

The reason to choose two countries, Japan and Finland as Parenting Models instead of ONE, is that there are two types of parenting styles: proximal and distal. In short, the proximal parenting style is associated with consistent and prolonged body contact between the mother and child, while the distal parenting style's emphasis is more on eye contact and communication through facial expression and words. Japan follows Distal Style, while Finland follows mainly Proximal Style of parenting.

Extraordinary Ways To Raise Your Parenting Eq

Being Parents - Premier Edition
Bhushan Khairnar
Child Growth Consultant and Investor

IBRN : 91012500412gfo4br
(International Blockchain based Book Registry System)
BBRS: 1676406

CHAPTER ONE

Experiencing the World

In Finland, Domestic tourism is largely dictated by children's needs, and child-friendly attractions abound in the height of summer, while winter brings its own snowy delights, including Santa.

Japanese children are taught to take focused and purposive experience of the world. Children at early age learn to move around city alone but not to just enjoy but to become self-reliant. The culture has allowed children to experience the real world by themselves. The experience of the real world is important to the children.

Science tells us that the experiences, we have in the first years of our lives, actually affect the physical architecture of the developing brain. This means that brains aren't just born. They're also built over time based on our experiences. Just as a house needs a sturdy foundation to support the walls and roof, a brain needs a good base to support all future development.

While designing experiences, you should consider primarily both the aspects of real world experiences - Psychological and Physical. The physical experiences has direct impact on brain architecture. Parents can design the experiences in three ways:

- Experiences in Daily Life
- Local Visits
- Travels

Experiences in Daily Life:

Conscious Interaction

Parents should interact more with their children. Not like mature to immature person. Children should not be taken for granted. They need your conscious attention and respect to grow positively. Parents should see their children as they are and matching their ways and styles, parents should interact with them.

Don't always be teacher or commanding officer towards them. Imagine a tennis match between a parents and a child but instead of hitting a ball back and forth across the net various forms of communication passed between the two from eye contact to touch, from singing to simple games like peek-a-boo these interactions repeated throughout a young person's developing years are the bricks that build a healthy foundation for all future development.

What and How you interact with your children is very important in their development. Positive interactions between young children and their parents literally build the architecture of the developing brain. Building a sturdy foundation in the earliest years provides a good base for a lifetime of good mental function and better overall health. So just how is a solid brain foundation built and maintained in a developing child one-way is through what brain experts call serve and return interactions.

Stress

There is another world beyond you and your family, the world outside. Interactions, meetings, activities, confrontations, physical world, behaviours of people, makes your children uncomfortable. It creates stress within them. How you transform those experiences into positive stress is very important being parents. Ignoring these portion may develop multiple fallacies into your children brain.

Good kinds of stress like meeting new people or studying for a test are healthy for development because they prepare kids to cope with future challenges. Another kind of stress, called toxic stress is bad for brain development. If a child is exposed to serious ongoing hardships like abuse and neglect and he has no other caregiver in his life to provide support, the basic structures of his developing brain may be damaged.

Plan ahead and remember and follow lots of rules like all of us, kids have to react to things happening in the world around them while also dealing with worries, temptations and obligations on their mind. As these demands for attention pile-up air traffic control helps a child regulate the flow of information prioritise tasks and above all find ways to manage stress and avoid mental collisions along the way.

Having this ability is a necessity for positive and level mental health. Developing affective air traffic control, overcoming toxic stress and building solid brain architecture are things kids can't do on their own and since strong societies are made up of healthy contributing individuals it's up to us as a community to make sure all young people have the kinds of nurturing experiences they need for positive development. To build better futures we need to build better brains.

You should consider their age, environment and choices while designing the experiences. You should also plan to teach them how to overcome negative experiences.

Local Visits

The world outside home is the new world for your children. It's opportunity to learn about the world for the children. Plan your local visits in a way that it covers various aspects of human life, routine life to historical places, entertainment to riverside life. Let your children experience them it themselves, let them observe, help them understand if they are puzzled. Only parent should be doing is to provide safety and security to the children in the environment.

The first step to plan local visits is to understand the local culture, events, geography and experiences at specific places.

Travel

Travelling provides them the broad view of the life, a chance to connect with global culture and practical experience of the real world.

The benefits of travel are absolutely endless – culture experiences, savoury flavours, breathtaking landscapes, new adventures and tightened family bonds, just to name a few. As a parent, to offer an experience like this from a young age can cultivate a passion for travel in children; a passion that plays a vital role in their development.

Real-world learning experiences, like summer trip to desert, can significantly improve children's knowledge in a matter of just days, a new study suggests. When you travel, think consciously and experience things yourself, it create a deep impact on their life.

One of the best things about travel is that it's a huge mind opener. "Individuals who have a broader understanding of 'the way things are', rather than the myopic outlook that can develop from vegetating in one little corner of the earth all one's lifetime", says Mark Twain. They thrive on it and soak everything up including languages and culture differences that become similarities.

From cultural awareness to diving head first into new and exciting experiences, travel can work wonders in the minds of young children. It's a scholastic way to broaden their minds through complete immersion – it beats learning in any classroom! And whilst it may seem like a hassle at first to travel with your little ones (especially under the age of 5!) it's an opportunity for them to receive a worldly education in context. An education even the youngest children can still benefit from.

Life is very different on the road that's part of its magic – it forces us to break away from those daily routines. Travelling with your children helps your young ones to accept new roles through decision making and skill development. This will teach them the value of packing and organising, decision making and accepting responsibility for their own things.

Throughout the travelling experience, your children can adapt to job roles like navigating on a map, finding an interesting place to visit or deciding on a place to eat. Both kids and parents will learn new skills through these roles and responsibilities from travel. And these are the sort of skills that will stay with them to adapt to other areas in life as they grow up.

Whether it's just you and your young one travelling together or it's a whole family trip, travelling is notorious for strengthening bonds. Bonds as a whole family, bonds between siblings, bonds between mother and daughter or father and son and better yet, bonds between you and your partner.

Families share a whole range of experiences together when traveling. And it's these experiences that enhance family bonds. Whether you're fishing with your son or teaching your daughter bravery through rock climbing, getting involved in a unique culture experience encourages a sense of fun and adventure together. Travel provides the perfect opportunity for you as a family to collect memories, not things.

Travel can bring out the worst and best in people so there's plenty of opportunities to practice valuable lessons. They'll learn to adapt to new situations, meet different challenges and be flexible enough to be patience in an unexpected lifestyle.

Waiting in long lines for a ride or tourist attraction, embarking on long flights and bus trips and group decision making can all provide opportunities for your children to speak up and learn from things. Practical decisions can be made as a family, problem solving and trip planning become good skills they can develop on.

Despite some parents believing that pulling children out of class to travel can mean lack of socialisation with others, it's quite the opposite. And even better, it allows them to connect with people all ages, all nationalities and all walks of life – people that can enrich their lives even further.

CHAPTER TWO

Health - Food and Activities

Japanese mums believe in meticulous meal planning, especially when it comes to their children's lunch boxes. They believe the right nutrition can help strengthen their immune system and will work wonders for their development.

Japanese mums make the effort to prepare elaborate multi-item meals. They also make sure that they are colourful enough to entice children so they eat every healthy item on the plate.

"Japanese moms set high standards for their children's bento box meals, rising early to prepare an elaborate selection of healthy items that look pretty too — fish, vegetables, tofu, seaweed, rice balls shaped like animals or plants,"

The most important thing that you can teach your kid about food is that food isn't just about taste. The primary purpose of food is not just to give you some sort of a euphoric sensual experience three times a day but it's not the primary purpose of food.

The primary purpose of food is to fuel your body. Just to give your body the proper balance of nutritional components that it needs to function at an optimal level. If you get that into a kid's head early on, that's going to put them on the right path for life.

This doesn't mean that food can't and shouldn't be pleasurable, colourful. It should be pleasurable but the primary purpose of eating and drinking is to fuel your body. When you see people who are in good physical shape, they're doing a good job with this. They get it when you see people who struggle in this area, they just haven't made that connection powerfully enough kids need to know this and it's their parents that should be teaching it to them.

Eating behaviours evolve during the first years of life; children learn what, when, and how much to eat through direct experiences with food and by observing the eating behaviours of others.

The first year of life is a period of rapid physical, social and emotional growth, during which eating patterns also develop. During this first year, infants transition from consuming a single food (i.e., breast milk or formula) to consuming a variety of foods more characteristic of an adult diet. This transition allows infants to learn about food through direct experience, as well as through observation of others' eating behaviours.

Infants are born with a preference for sweet and salty taste, thus sweet and salty foods have a greater likelihood of being accepted by infants when compared to foods with bitter flavours, such as certain vegetables. Both infants and young children can learn to accept a greater variety of foods and flavours through repeated exposure.

Parents who are concerned about their child's diet may attempt to limit what and how much food is eaten, pressure their child to eat a healthier diet, or reward their child for eating healthy foods, practices which may all lead to unintended consequences.

Over the years we've seen three fundamental reasons why people fail in this area. I have discovered that failure in this category comes down to one or more of the three following mindsets:

- I don't know
- I don't care
- I can't help myself

Let's take a closer look at these three mindsets the first is I don't know - ignorant - I literally don't know that - How much bread is good, what is the best time to give fruits to my child, milk is good or curd? Horlicks is better or bournvita? Veg- Sandwich is good or pizza? And so many questions.What quantity, what qualities and what products are good for my children's health?

I don't know while I'm sitting on the sofa, watching TV is not a good wellness strategy while eating. I just don't know.

The second mindset for failure is I don't care. Laziness which really comes down to apathy. It simply means I know that stuff's not good for my children but I just don't care enough to change their behavior or children are not easy to convince.

I just don't care that's a bad road to get trapped on that is a recipe for disaster.

The third reason that people fail in the category of health and fitness of their children is that I can't help myself. You have no sufficient knowledge about food or How to change the food habits of children or there is no authentic source to tell me what food is best suitable to my children. So, I can't help it, I know this behavior is bad. I know it's self-destructive and I really do care. I wish I could stop it but I can't seem to help myself. I know I shouldn't be doing it but I'd do it anyway and this one sucks. This one is so bad because there's all kinds of negative painful emotions like shame and guilt involved in this one and those hurt lack of self esteem.

You can literally do amazing. You gain knowledge, plan, make a habit, observe which food is good and which doesn't for your children and repeat.

I have discovered over the years you can either continue to struggle with one or more of these issues in your life, with one or more of these mindsets for failure or you can literally transcend them and take them out of play simply by getting your purpose on in this category.

Always remember, in order to be a good parent you've got to set a good example for your kids. That's the number one job of a parent to show your kids what it looks like, to have a healthy happy successful life and taking good care of your body is critical to being a good parent. So, teaching your kids about health, teaching your kids about nutrition and exercise, it's one of our primary responsibilities. If we want to be extraordinary parents and I will tell you that this is an area where we're seeing parents fail more and more over the years.

Here are few tips to help you create a positive eating environment for your children.

Have regular and Fix meal and snack times

Having regular meal and snack times everyday creates a healthy routine. If your children eat whenever they feel like it, they may not be hungry when it's time for a scheduled meal or snack. They may also overeat during the day.

Eat together as a family - Children shall copy what parents eat.

Children who eat meals with their family tend to eat healthier foods like fruits, vegetables and whole grains. They are also at lower risk for becoming overweight. However, children who eat in front of the TV tend to make poorer food choices. Eating meals in front of the TV should be avoided as this can lead to overeating and a higher risk of childhood obesity.

Avoid pressuring your children to eat

Insisting that your children eat certain foods may actually cause them to eat less. As a parent, you are responsible for providing healthy food choices to your children. Your children should be allowed to decide how much to eat based on how hungry they feel. Habit formation is a collaborative task.

Avoid using food as a reward or punishment

Eating is a way to nourish our bodies. Using food as a reward or punishment may lead to unhealthy eating habits. Offer a variety of healthy foods and let your children serve themselves without any pressure.

Have healthy foods at home

Gain enough knowledge about healthy food and ensure to buy the healthy food from the market. The foods available in your fridge, freezer, cupboards and pantry are what your children will get used to eating.

Parents are role models

Parents can influence their children's eating habits in a positive way by being a good role model. Here are some tips on how to be a good role model when it comes to food.

Make healthy foods the usual choice

What you eat sets an example for what your children will eat. Enjoy variety of foods such as vegetables, fruit, whole grain products, low fat dairy products, lean meats, legumes, eggs and fish. When your children see you eating these foods, they are more likely to want to eat them too.

Limit foods high in calories, fat, sugar and salt

Foods that are high in calories, fat, sugar and salt like cakes, chocolate, cookies, doughnuts, ice cream, French fries, potato chips, pop, sports and energy drinks, and sweetened hot or cold drinks should be eaten less often. When you limit these foods yourself, your children will be less likely to eat them as well. It is important not to label these foods as "bad". They are simply foods to be eaten occasionally and in moderation.

As a parent, you have an important role in shaping your children's eating habits. By creating a positive eating environment and being a good role model, you can help your children develop healthy eating habits that can make a lasting impact on their health.

CHAPTER THREE

Teach them about Money

In Finland and Japan, the values are given the first priority. They believe money is only a medium to transfer values. If you serve someone, you are rewarded. Money means productivity, helping others and doing things meticulously.

It is parents' job to teach their children about Money. It's not about only sending them to corporate schools, preparing them for exams and get them better jobs. I don't say - these categories are not important but usually parents miss out on majority of important factors about money.

It's so unbelievable, we go to school for almost two decades and we learn about everything else but not about money. If we don't teach your kids about the creation of wealth, no one will you can. We go to school for years or more and we learn about Geography, Algebra, Geometry, Maths, Chemistry, History, Sociology, Literature, Music, Computers, Art and we learn to do home-work. We complete our schoolings and then we graduate and we get more certificates and finally, we spend the majority of our waking hours, just about every day, for the rest of our lives, trying to make MONEY. And the money subject, we've learned absolutely nothing about in school and colleges.

Parents have little idea how to make their children financially responsible and build their career around their interest. They have unclear idea about MONEY. I believe the following explanation will help parents to understand and make them able to teach their children about money.

I developed a deep understanding of what money is, where it comes and how people viewed money. People perceive it very wrong - what wealth is, where it comes from and what it can do for people.

Let's start with this question - "what is money?"

Money is simply a tool of trade. It's a medium of exchange, nothing more nothing less. Money is an invention that allows us to trade the goods, we create and the services we offer, more easily. It's one of the most important inventions in the history of our species.

Without money, civilization would not have even been possible. Money has two primary purposes -

1. to standardize value so that people can trade things more easily and
2. to store value so that people can save it and trade it at a later date

And these two things are the foundation of the civilized world. Here's an example of what standardizing value means - Imagine, I was a wheat farmer, a few thousand years ago before money was invented, I want some eggs. well I'm gonna have to barter. I need to find a guy with chickens and try to trade him some wheat for some eggs. But if the chicken guy doesn't want wheat and he demand that he wants beef. Now I am going to find a guy with cows and if I find the guy with cows, but he doesn't want my wheat either. He says that he wants three clay pots and now I'm gonna have to find a Potter, so finally, the Potter is willing to trade me three pots for my wheat. So now, I can trade the pots for the beef and the beef for the eggs.

That's what people used to have to do to trade their goods and services. They had to trade their stuff directly for other people's stuff and it was really clumsy.

Money got rid of all that. Money allowed me to turn my wheat into silver coins and those coins were recognized as the standard of value by everyone. I could trade them for eggs or beef or three pots or jewelry for my wife, anything I wanted in one step. It's more efficient.

Money is a medium of exchange. Money standardizes or equalizes value. It makes everything worth X amount of these little things. Money also allowed people to store value.

Earlier, as a wheat farmer I work all year long in my fields but the harvest happens all at once. If I don't trade my wheat quickly it's gonna mould and all my work is gonna go down the drain. So I have to trade it for whatever is available at the time. If I want to trade my wheat for a horse but there's none available at the time too bad for me. May be next year, there's gonna be a horse available, when I have some more wheat.

Money changed all that - with money. I can turn my wheat into coins and then I can trade those coins not only for what I want, when I want and even I can wait a month, a year and even pass that money on to my children. Money allowed people to save and what is it that we're saving.

Money is stored energy. Today we use paper money. We use Dollars. Dollars are pieces of paper printed by the government. By themselves, they're worthless. You can't eat them, you can't live in them, you can't do anything with them, other than what they were invented for - trade products and services.

It's not the Dollar themselves that have worth. It's only what the Dollar represent.

Why is this important to understand stop chasing those pieces of paper and focus on what they represent. You'll find out that Money represents the very best things that people have to offer each other, the goods and the services that people produce. With money people can easily exchange their work, their talents, their skills.

Money is literally a symbol of human productivity and achievement. It represents all the good things that we create for each other. Today we trade our work for money which we then use to trade for the work of other people.

Steven Spielberg his work is to make movies and the rest of us go to work and we trade our various talents and skills for money and then we trade a small part of what we've earned with Steven Spielberg's company. So that we can enjoy an evening entertainment. The value Bill Gates has created is software. That's changed the way that people live and he's wealthy because he's positively affected the lives of literally billions of people. A doctor, a teacher, a lawyer a janitor, they all provide valuable services to other people. They exchange those services for money, so they can acquire the valuable services of others.

You trade your work for money. When you are better at what you do, the more valuable you become and the more money you can trade. Your work for money is a symbol of the best that people have to offer each other.

Should we love money?

If it mean little green pieces of paper with pictures of dead president on them, the answer is NO. But if money is what it represents, the answer is absolutely YES.

You should teach your children at a very young age that money is a symbol of human productivity and human achievement that represents all the good things that people create and that it's absolutely worthy of your respect and your admiration.

Teach that wealth, progress, prosperity or what eliminate poverty and human suffering is the highest form of contribution. If you've been encouraged by everyone around you to develop and apply your unique talents to the pursuit and the creation of wealth, how might your life be different than it is right now.

Your beliefs and your attitudes toward money and wealth and have a major impact on whether or not you're going to be able to create financial abundance in your life and how you think about money will determine your financial condition.

Wealth is created by creating value for your fellow human beings. On the other side of the coin, the money concept is surrounded by so much stress, so much confusion and just so much weirdness.

Stephen Covey says ***"The main thing is to keep the main thing, the main thing ,"*** Happiness is the main thing if your mission is to create a truly extraordinary life of your children or yours'.

The money is necessary ingredient to make life happy and fulfilling. Always remember, Money is a stored value.

CHAPTER FOUR

Set Safe and Secure Environment (Physical and Psychological)

Finland and Japan are the most safest country in the world for children. In Japan, children were encouraged to be self-reliant. They are taught to do their work by their own from very early age. In Finland, Young people in Finland usually move away from home after coming of age when they begin studying or find a job. It is common for them to live either alone or with student friends before starting a family.

A successful parenting is about making sure that your kids can function in your absence. They can function successfully without you. That's your big mission. And by the way, that just doesn't just apply to humans, it applies to all creatures. Whether you're a duck or a deer or basically any organism on this earth parenting is a race to get your kids ready for life.

Before something eats them right or before they fly the coop or before they go out there into the world and forge their own path as parents, we got to help them become autonomous. That's our number one job to get them to the point where they can function successfully in our absence.

It's up to us to create a safe sane loving environment in which our children can really thrive the most critical factor in a child's development is safety - physical, psychological, emotional and intellectual safety.

Their physical safety is first and foremost keeping them from getting hurt, keeping them out of danger, making sure they have proper food, clothing and shelter. Then comes psychological safety. Children need the experience of living in a rational universe a world in which facts are treated as facts, truth is respected, question asking is valued and not punished. An environment in which a child's desire to understand is honored and nurtured.

Our primary role as parents is to make sure that our children possess the competence to cope with the challenges of life when we're not there to guide them. So we've got to help them become self-sufficient. We've got to equip them with the skills and the tools, they need to navigate their own life in the way they see fit to develop a sense of efficacy and to learn to trust themselves to make good decisions for their own lives.

The single most important thing that we can teach our children is "You are the author of your own life. "

It's difficult to have to give them a little more freedom every single year. You know to let them make their own choices to let them make their own mistakes and to constantly be resisting the temptation to jump in and solve all their problems for them but at the end of the day from a cosmic perspective.

You need to teach them to make their own decisions and choices. And make them understand that the life they are going to get is a result of those decisions and those choices.

Their life is a result of their daily choices and actions what they do with the minutes and the hours and the days of their life. It dictates who they are becoming and what kind of a life they will have. That's the most important thing that we can teach our kids.

Parents can't be there to make every one of their decisions for them. They are in control of your their own existence. Now helping our kids become autonomous, doesn't mean that parents let them run rampant and live without rules and just do whatever they want.

They've got a lot of rules in the same way that we want them to understand that they own their lives and we own our lives. And this is our house and as long as they live in our house they are going to live by our rules.

We want to let children enjoy the wonder of childhood. We want them to be carefree, we want them to be silly and happy. It's super important to us. But what it does mean is that we instill in them from a very young age that we do not own them, they own themselves. We're just temporarily in charge of them and helping them to learn and grow, taking care of them, nurturing them. We make it clear that we're going to do that as long as it takes to get them ready to go out into the world and someday to create their own extraordinary life for themselves.

CHAPTER FIVE

Career - How to choose and grow

The freedom to choose and think is the first priority of Finnish parents. The practical Education and training is valued in Finland and parents' encouragement. In Finland and Japan, what actually parents think, what parents believe from inside, and how they implement it is more important.

Career of your children is the most important priority as a parents. We desire our children to live happy and in financial abundance. There are many misconceptions about career among parents - higher education, better jobs, good grades at schools, various entrance exams, etc defines their children's career. It doesn't mean these exams and jobs are useless. But that's not the complete truth. The people with successful career and fulfilling life has something else in common.

Career is not a single event. The process of building successful career starts from very early age. The career process starts when you choose something to do yourself for the first time in the life as a toddler.

The clarity about what you choose to do is the first step towards successful and happy career. Parents need to support their children to make independent choices rather enforced or guided by some authority. When other decides what you should do, there are rare chances that you shall be happy doing the things for rest of your life.

We learn gradually what we enjoy and what activities we don't. What you enjoy doing, you gradually become better at doing it. Hence, parents should expose their children to the various activities so that they develop broader capacities to analyse their opportunities to choose and execute.

When toddlers play, they like the positive responses from the people around them. The sense of involving and affecting the world around is natural to human being. The better you do your job, the better you receive -

the understanding is natural.

The environment which allows children to share and connect with outside world will prepare them for sharing their talents openly and create their space in the real world.

For further clarity, let's start with what our research of thousands of people:

We live in an age of unprecedented opportunity when it comes to career we have a wider range of choices than ever before in human history. There are hundreds of professions that didn't even exist a few decades ago. You can choose just about any career you want. It hasn't always been that way. So what's the result of all this wonderful opportunity information overload. Most of us are just completely overwhelmed. There are too many choices but it's also bewildering and confusing with all the possibilities.

There are a few common-sense things that we can consider. No one wants to spend the hours of their life doing something they don't like. So it makes good sense to pick something you like something you enjoy.

It also makes sense to pick something "you're good at" or "could be good at" because it doesn't make any sense to spend your life doing something that you don't have the aptitude to do well. That would be frustrating you don't want to work for years and not get better. If you pick something your natural at, you'll get better and better over time.

The next consideration is financial abundance. The vast majority of us want careers that make us the most money possible.

Contribute to others at the highest level of which we're capable. The greater our contribution is, the greater our financial rewards are. Parents can help their children from choosing career to successful and fulfilling career by making them understanding the following three things:

- First - I must choose something I love
- Second - I must get good at it and
- Third - I must make a significant contribution to others if I want to create financial abundance.

The first step is to find work you love. Discover what's inside of you, that's the best and highest possible use. Find your unique talent and then develop it. This needs practice. It doesn't just fall out of the sky and into your life but if you can discover - what you could be great at. Then apply yourself. That's the beginning of your dream career. Loving your work just gives you a huge advantage.

You want to get out of bed every morning and go to work. You bring passion, joy and enthusiasm to your work that creates energy. When you have passion for your work, every day is exciting, every day is a joy, every day is a blessing and you automatically bring a new level of thinking to your work. When you love what you do, success tends to come naturally.

The second step is to get really good at what you do. Develop competence, develop expertise. If you're competent, if you're an expert at your job that means you can deliver the goods. If you're good at what you do, people will seek you out. They'll want to deal with you. You'll be more successful.

Being good at what you do, gives you self-esteem. You feel good about yourself which makes you want to do even better. I think that everyone has the potential to have a fulfilling career because everyone has the potential to be good at something. We all have the capacity to develop a valuable, unique talent or ability.

The third step is to find a way to contribute. Find the need and fill it when you can match your talent to the needs of others. That's the way to create wealth. If you make yourself valuable to people, they're going to pay you for what you do. Ask yourself - What can I contribute people with? How can I use my talent to help others people?

People who are wealthy have discovered and developed their talents and figured out how to match those talents to the needs of others.

You can literally pick a career that you like and then you can learn about it and get good at it and trade the fruits of your labor for the fruits of labor of others. That's pretty amazing.

Not all of us not every career directly involves creating wealth. Being a stay-at-home parent for instance, it's a fantastic career. Running the household right, you've got to be a chauffeur, a psychologist, a nurse, a housekeeper, a teacher and more but that career doesn't earn money directly.

CHAPTER SIX

Quality Way of Thinking

Thinking is primarily an act of analysing and creating meaning out of the received information, situations we are in, environment we create and choose, the choices we make in our day to day life, how we deal with people and based on the perception, the actions we take.

The quality of your children's lives will be based to a huge extent on their ability to think in a high quality way. Parents should teach how to think while schools teaches what to think.

Thinking is an internal mental process. If you see a chess player engrossed in thinking for several minutes before making a move, you cannot observe what he is thinking. You can simply infer what he was thinking or what strategies he was trying to evaluate, from his next move.

Parents should understand one fact that Thinking is a CHOICE. As a human being, we have rights to choose whether to think or not. You decide whether to think about a particular matter or not. Nobody can force you to think.

Even though thinking is a natural process, the quality of thinking gets better as we practice. The quality way of thinking involves -

- What we choose to think
- How we think (Interpret the information), what resources we choose and with what clarity
- Plan of Action

Through out the day, we make multiple choices based on what kind of life we desire. When the goals are clear, we know what to think about. The choices are based on our conscious thinking process, what kind of life we desire, what we need to do to live our desired life. How small, everyday actions are going to affect our life visions - if we understand this, it's become easy to choose what we should think about. Instead of letting others like TV commercial tells you what mobile to choose, we should think, build your own vision for our better life.

Parenting is about helping their children understand the life goals in clear ways and in accordance with them, make choices about daily activities.

Second step, human being learn things from other human beings. The first mobile phone are so different than today's smart phones. By learning from other human beings, we grow as human species. But imagine, if your TV is not working properly, will you approach motor Garage or TV repairing shop? The answer is obvious but for new and complex problems, the choice of the resource become difficult.

Hence, parents need to teach their children how to make better choices and how to identify the better resources to solve the problem. That can be done by giving them daily home based responsibilities to real world exposures based on their age and capacities. Teach them how to approach resources, connect with other people and make things happens in favour of you.

There might be many tasks to be done in a day or a week. To prioritise actions, planning and clarity is essential. What comes first? Parents need to teach their children about saying NO to certain things and giving priority to few.

We can say, ***Thinking means the quality of life that you choose consciously.***

CHAPTER SEVEN

Self-Expression

In Finland, children spends just three hours in the classroom. And every afternoon, they have time for free play. The children are free to explore life and become self-reliant.

Expression refers to the ways in which a child communicates their thoughts, ideas, knowledge and feelings. Through their bodies, words and use of materials, children develop increasingly complex communications skills.

When an infant cries, it extend its hands to tell that "*I am Hungry, I need your attention.*" Self-expression is a very basic need of human being. As we grow, the ways of expressing self changes and get more polished.

Self-Expression is about everything you do and say. Expressing yourself means finding a way to show your feelings, thoughts and ideas through creative play such as arts and crafts, dance, photography, drama, music and writing.

Self-Expression means all the opportunities that you have to express yourself from the clothes you put on, in the morning to the share posts on social media, to share your success stories with your friends at night.

The journey fo self-expression starts from survival need and gets mature to collaborative value exchange. Creating our own space in the world and creating impact on it are our natural desires just like kids cry to get toy.

Parents should allow children to explore possibilities and express themselves freely. Take an example, when your children are playing and trying to put ball into bowl, do you help them to do it? Let them find the way. Motivation can create positive impact on them but it's okay if they move on and try something else. "Our job as a parent is simple, Creating possibilities for new experiences and explorations."

Through play, children develop the ability to express their ideas, to think and imagine. Just imagine, toys that are actually expected to use just in a certain way or are we providing them with materials that allow a wide range of possibilities but they put an extra layer of imagination to it. Even just commenting on what's happening - saying, "Wow" look, this is really rewarding to children.

One of the ways to support children's coping is to support in visualizing - what they're feeling and what they're thinking. Whether through painting things, building small models or being able to express through music or dance supporting children's active physical forms of play, basically wire their brains with positive experiences that last not only to school but throughout the lifetime.

Allow your children to express their own way. You might not be comfortable initially but ensure, they have enough freedom to express themselves their ways.

Self-expression is crucial for the development of a child's identity, self-confidence and sense of belonging to the world. It opens children's minds and allows them to form thoughts and ideas. Self-expression helps children communicate their feelings in a positive way.

The world needs Authentic self-expression. It doesn't need another Warren Buffet, Steve Jobs or Oprah Winfrey. It needs individuals, their gifts, their talents, their unique expression.

CHAPTER EIGHT

Managing Emotional and Rational Life

Japanese parents understand that emotional well-being of a child is as significant as his physical well-being. Scolding a kid and making him realise his mistake is important but that should not be done in a harsh manner as that may affect the child's mental health.

Danish psychotherapist Iben Sandahl,"*The Danish Way of Parenting: A Guide To Raising The Happiest Kids in the World*" says that the Danish parents believe - Before we can be good at recognizing the emotions of others, we have to be able to understand our own emotions. Parents sometimes tell children what they think they should or shouldnt feel. They override them. If they are sad, angry, hungry, cold, or upset, some parents tell them, "No, you aren't, Dont be sad, You have no reason to be angry, You should be hungry, eat!" Telling children how they should feel is not letting them learn to self-regulate their own feelings. As parents, we have to give our children trust so that they can learn about their own emotional boundaries. This builds a stronger sense of self, which is paramount to self-esteem down the road. When they are older they will be less afraid to say no when their boundaries are pushed because they will trust themselves to make the right decision based on what they feel. This is such an important lesson to teach children. We can help them with the language use, but we need to trust them so they can trust themselves. Remember, there are no good or bad emotions. There are just emotions.

Healthy emotional life is indispensable for living a happy successful life. Aristotle said, "Happiness is the most important thing in the world." If you ask yourself why you want anything you want in life enough times, you're gonna come up with one final answer - ***"because I want to be happy."***

For majority of parents, there is absolutely no clue how to understanding feelings and emotions of their children. Their game plan is usually going to be - I'll just keep them happy all the time because it's really easy to keep your turfy all the time and it is impossible, it's it's ridiculous. It's incredibly exhausting trying to keep people happy all the time.

There are three ways how parents deal with feelings and emotions in wrong way:

The first one is repression. It means that as a child if you learnt that it wasn't safe to express your feelings. Perhaps you got shut down, you were told to stop crying. Perhaps you were given a look that made you draw everything inside, then you were going to have to find a way to cope with all those feelings and emotions. The most of the people learned to repress them. They push them down deep. Most of the times, they disassociated.

The second thing is authoritarian environment. When a children grew up in an authoritarian environment, where they didn't have a voice, where they couldn't say how we felt, then those feelings again would bubble inside them. And at the point, where they would tip over. When they often felt frightened or threatened, they would come out in aggression in rage, in loud words and sometimes they might have been labeled as naughty, too much or trouble. In fact, all you were doing was responding to your environment. Then as adults those aggression tendencies turn up in bullying behavior. They turn up in harsh critical thoughts about themselves and others they turn up as violence.

The third thing is no freedom to expression. It means that if children grow up in an environment where they are not allowed to express their own way, their feelings are not accepted, their thoughts are not respected and when they are not listened, they grow suppressed. They find it difficult to adjust in the world. They are unable to express their skills and their emotions.

To avoid these mistakes and deal better way with the challenge, here are few simple steps to teach your children to have healthy emotional life. There are two things you can teach them to keep them emotionally happy and responsible.

First, to create environment where children can express feelings freely, without fear of rejection. Encourage them to be honest with themselves and express and accept their all positive and negative emotions.

Second, teach them to create emotional environment consciously. Just as you make them happy by playing the music that they like. Explore various ways to create such environment. Teach them that they have power to create happy environment around them. Teach them to be responsible for their being happy or unhappy, be satisfied or not, be positive or negative by asking them to do it for themselves during their childhood.

Rational Life:

We're not obligated to monitor the beating of our hearts that happens automatically but when it comes to thinking, nature has given us an extraordinary responsibility. According to some scientists, the ability to think rationally by the age of seven.

Hence, parents should start exposing to their children to the world at very early age. Let them take experiences and developing rational thinking.

The world around us functions rationally. If you jump from height, you are going down. There are hardcore principles based on which world respond to you. Just like the law of physics, the world mirrors on you.

So, our ability to think is what keeps us alive. Everything we have in our civilization from computers to mail boxes, from refrigerators to books, the chair you're sitting on, the clothes we are wearing, everything was brought into existence by the process of thinking for humans.

The principle reflected in our every aspect of life. If you desire better job, you need to prove your abilities to deliver better values than other candidates.

Everything starts with a thought. Every great work of art, every building, every invention, everything in our entire civilisation began with a thought and was brought into existence through a process of thinking and in exactly the same way everything in your life began with a thought.

We live in a world that requires us to navigate through a jungle of information on a daily basis. The news we read, the content we see online and the people we interact with, all shape how we view the world. This inevitably influences the choices that we make: from the food we eat and the music we listen to, to our attitudes towards the environment and the political candidates we vote for.

To make informed decisions, we must shift through a deluge of information. To determine which claims are supported by evidence and which are not. Hard as it may be, we sometimes have to be willing to abandon some of our most deeply rooted views, when confronted with evidence to the contrary.

Being rational is not the same as being clever as a fox, though. Even the smartest of us can act irrationally. Sometimes we may simply not care what the evidence shows. Or perhaps we want to win an argument instead of seeking the truth. And some of us may be perfectly happy to base our decisions on what the majority of our group thinks, without reviewing the evidence ourselves.

We, humans, are highly social animals after all: we live in families, have circles of friends and are members of society. So even though we are capable of thinking on our own, we do it much more often in the company of others. Taking all of this into account will allow us to move towards a society that is able to reason collectively. It can help to prevent polarization, build consensus and ultimately contribute to a healthy democracy.

To develop better rational life of your children, you need to understand one fact - We literally have a choice to think or not to think and the other half is choosing what to think about.

CHAPTER NINE

Setting Goals and Achieving them

The point of life when your child desire something, his journey to learn the way of setting and achieving starts. When child wants a toy, it is setting goal for himself/herself. The child starts crying and stops walking, are its efforts to achieve the goal.

Parents's job is to understand their children's desires and convert those desires into goals by interacting with their children or making it price-game process. It shall lead you and your children towards setting smart goals, planning and achieving them for broader purposes of life.

Parents should know the fact that the children set the basic neurological structure within 5-6 years of their age. It means, early they learn about the goal setting and achieving process help them succeed with ease.

Setting Goals

People who set goals, know exactly what they want and take actions to achieve it. When you're doing what it takes to achieve your goals, you're moving towards the lifestyle that you desire. In order to set goals, you need to think about what you want in every aspect of life - Family relationship, friends, health and fitness, finances, career, education, spirituality, self-development and any other aspects.

When you set your goals, it's important to do it in a smart way. The smart acronym is a popular method used in business and personal development. In the setting of different objects in our goals:

- S stands for specific
- M for measurable

- A is attainable
- R is relevant and
- T means time bound

Parents need to teach their children, how to set a clear Short term and Long term goals. They should teach them the ways to gain clarity about exactly what their children desire. Prepare detailing and create a clear mental picture about goal is the first step.

Second step will be to set measurable goal, not generalise goals like I want better health instead I shall loose 1 pound in 15 days. Break your goal into measurable elements that you can keep on track and measure. Your progress measurement will let you know when you achieve your goal. A non measurable goal would be like I live a healthy lifestyle, while a measurable one would be I go to the gym three times a week, stick to my diet and meditate every day.

Third step to set attainable goals. The goals you set should be not very difficult and not so simple. You need to stay realistic. If you want to workout two hours a day, but you're a single parent who works many hours, you'll be hard to achieve in this case. You can set a different goal, maybe half an hour a day or find a creative solution like taking the stairs instead of the elevator or use a bicycle instead of driving.

The fourth step is to set relevant goal. The goal should have clear purpose and in relation to your life. Example - if you wish to have a wife and five children but you're still in high school, it is a goal that's relevant for the future but not for now and you can focus on other things like getting better understanding about science law or how electricity is produced.

The final step to set goal is to stay time-bounded. If you don't set deadlines for your goals, you lose momentum and procrastinate. When your goals are time bound, you get a sense of urgency and start to work. It may be hard to set a deadline for a long term goal, so you can start with setting deadlines for your sub goals, try not to set deadlines that are too far. Setting priority is effective practice. For example, I'd like to travel around the world for a year but it's your 12th standard and desire to achieve good ranks. Your goal list should be clear and with priorities, you are able to focus one thing at one time. Don't set multiple tasks at a time.

Achieving Goals

Ideas aren't worth anything, without the ability to execute those ideas, without the ability to bring those ideas into reality. And this is where, the most people fall apart in implementation. Very few people know, how to take purposeful effective intelligent action toward their goals every single day

The same applies to your children. If they don't learn how to achieve the set goals, their life will not be as per their desired vision. The greatest visions in the world are useless unless they can be implemented effectively. What really matters is that you achieve the life that you design.

Not knowing how to effectively implement is the number one thing that holds people back and keeps people broke and frustrated and stuck. There's a massive amount of misinformation out there, filling people's heads with ideas like to get-rich-quick, schemes magic pills, irrational philosophies everyone's selling a shortcut to getting what you want out of life.

The miracle diets that claim that you can eat as much as you want and still lose weight or the late-night infomercials that promise you wealth not based on the principles of wealth creation or the self-help guru that tells you that you can wish your way to your life vision. You can wish it into existence by just sitting around thinking all day and cheques will magically show up in the mail. These ideas are harmful and they're dangerous.

You don't need a magic pill, you don't need a guru. You need to teach your children to stand on their own two feet, trust their own judgment and their own intelligence. They need to be the primary driving force behind every goal of revision, every desire that they have expressed in their life.

Do remember once your children know what they want out of their life. The next question is what are they going to do about it? What causes do they need to put in motion to create the effect. So the next step is to develop a plan that outlines what it's going to take to achieve their vision, dream.

Start with setting one clear goal can literally change the trajectory of your life. If your children learn this skill of setting goals and achieving them, their life will be far happy and successful.

Abraham Lincoln said, ***"A goal properly set is halfway reached".***

CHAPTER TEN

Managing Digital Life

In Finland, as the child reaches 4th Grade, they have their own cell-phone. Most of them have at the First-Grade.

The changes happening in the world are inevitable. The digital life or the virtual world is becoming as real as the physical world.

Many experts and analysts are unable to see through the real issue and addressing only half reality about the digital world. They see the digital world as positive and negative only.

The digital world is only replica of our physical world. It has provided larger space for Human Imagination, so, we find many new and uncomfortable life over there. This is the reason why children gets fast addicted to the digital media. Their imaginations are far more free than ours. In the process of growth, somehow we have lost the capacity to imagine the world with own free eyes but fortunately children haven't.

First of all, parents need to accept the change. For parents, the digital world is also a new experience. They themselves are in the process of understanding and exploring it. So, it has become absolutely difficult for them to see it with hawk-eye and guide their children to manage their digital life.

Instead of getting stunned with the virtual world, see it with rational eye. It's like our physical world which is half positive half negative, depending on how we choose to make it. Again it's about your choices and experiences. Children desire to see the world from digital devices, desire to experience the life from different types of people and cultures.

Parents have fear of gray world they might get exposed to, the addiction they might fall in, significant risks to children's safety, privacy and well-being, magnifying threats and harms and same as they might in the physical world. Parents should be concerned about these issues equally for both the world.

Now, You have additional responsibilities than your parents had. You have to develop positive habits for both the world and teach to balance their digital and physical life. You can't allow others to decide your children's life whether it's digital or physical world. Here are few steps, you can take to manage digital life of your children in efficient way:

Design Rules to Experience the Digital world. Just as physical world, plan digital experiences for all life categories. The new life of imagination should also have some space but not without purpose. Digital Media should work for you and within your family values and parenting style. When used thoughtfully and appropriately, media can enhance daily life. But when used inappropriately or without thought, media can displace many important activities such as face-to-face interaction, family-time, outdoor-play, exercise, unplugged downtime and sleep.

Treat media as you would do with any other environment in your child's life. The same parenting guidelines apply in both real and virtual environments. Set limits; kids need and expect them. Know your children's friends, both online and off. Know what platforms, software, and apps your children are using, what sites they are visiting on the web, and what they are doing online.

Do it together. Just like physical world, do digital activities together. Co-view, co-play and co-engage with your children when they are using screens— it encourages social interactions, bonding, and learning. Play a video game with your kids. It's a good way to demonstrate good sportsmanship and gaming etiquette. Watch a show with them; you will have the opportunity to introduce and share your own life experiences and perspectives—and guidance. Don't just monitor them online—interact with them, so you can understand what they are doing and be a part of it.

Values. Teach them that just like in physical world, our behaviours and manners are necessary part of digital interaction. Show them the ways, model to show how to do it. Because children are great mimics, limit your own media use. In fact, you'll be more available for and connected with your children if you're interacting, hugging and playing with them rather than simply staring at a screen.

Teach them how both worlds can go together rather creating border lines between them. You need to make your child understand that it's about choosing better over inferior. To watch zoo on YouTube delivers inferior experience than to actually visiting it and see the animals physically. I mean here that you need to make them comfortable in switching between both the world and make better choices.

It's OK for your teen to be online. Online relationships are part of typical adolescent development. Social media can support teens as they explore and discover more about themselves and their place in the grown-up world. Just be sure your teen is behaving appropriately in both the real and online worlds. Many teens need to be reminded that a platform's privacy settings do not make things actually "private" and that images, thoughts, and behaviors teens share online will instantly become a part of their digital footprint indefinitely. Keep lines of communication open and let them know you're there if they have questions or concerns.

Warn children about the importance of privacy and the dangers of predators and sexting. Teens need to know that once content is shared with others, they will not be able to delete or remove it completely, and includes texting of inappropriate pictures. They may also not know about or choose not to use privacy settings, and they need to be warned that sex offenders often use social networking, chat rooms, e-mail, and online gaming to contact and exploit children.

Mistakes are Obvious. Just like Physical world allow your children make mistakes using digital media. Try to handle errors with empathy and turn a mistake into a teachable moment. But some indiscretions, such as sexting, bullying, or posting self-harm images, may be a red flag that hints at trouble ahead. Parents must observe carefully their children's behaviors and, if needed, enlist supportive professional help, including the family pediatrician.

CHAPTER ELEVEN

Social Life

Social life is about your family, relatives, friends and mentors. The quality of relationship is essential in all over development of human being. Social life is about what kind of relationships do you want to develop in your social life. What kind of a relationship do you want to have with your family. How close do you want to be to them. Do you see yourself getting together and hanging out with your family on a regular basis. Maybe more than you do now. What kind of friends do you want to have. What kind of a friend do you want to be.

Our relationship with our family and with our friends now since relationships are about relating they're a moving target. They don't stay the same over time. They're dynamic. They're not static. They move and they fluctuate and as we'll see in order to be fulfilling and meaningful our relationships are going to take continuous energy and continuous care. They take an investment.

We often take our friends and family for granted. I mean we don't tend to give enough thought to what we really want out of these important relationships or what we need to bring to the table ourselves. But these relationships of ours, they're so important to living a complete and fulfilled life. They deserve some thought and attention.

What parents need to teach their children about Friendship:

First, You have to pick good friends. There are a lot of people to choose from and you should choose consciously and choose wisely. You become like your friends. So Don't hang out with people, you don't want to be like. Being selective is important because relationships take a significant investment of time and energy.

Secondly, You not only have to select good friends, You've got to be a good friend. You've got to ask yourself, "Am I the kind of a friend?" Being a good friend entails always being there lending a helping hand, sharing in the joys and helping through the tough times. You want your friends to be able to count on you in both the good times and the bad. You want to help them meet their needs. You want to be a giving friend in every sense of the word. You want to operate with kindness and compassion in your relationships. Pay compliments whenever you can make your friends feel good, make them feel important and loved and supported.

What kind of a relationship do you want to have with your family members? Do you need to spend more time with them than you do right now? Do you need to forge a stronger bond?

Just like friendship, you need to spend time and energy for better bonding. It's about give and take. You are ultimately dealing with human beings who have negative and positive vibes. You choose people who creates the environment around your children. Now you decide what sort of environment is better for your children growth.

CHAPTER TWELVE

Implementing Parenting Goals

"Mistakes are a part of life, irrespective of whether we try or not. However, an action is integral to moving forward, is it not? "

- Tony Robbins

The frontal lobes are important for voluntary movement, expressive language and for managing higher level executive functions. Executive functions refer to a collection of cognitive skills including the capacity to plan, organise, initiate, self-monitor and control one's responses in order to achieve a goal.

The most important reason that our brains insist on thinking about the future, even though sometimes we'd rather just kind of be here and frolic in the moment is so that we can exercise control over our world. Every great accomplishment was first imagined before it was implemented.

The most important reason that we set goals, we visualize our future because we can do something about it.

As human beings we have a deep need to have an effect on the world around us to influence things to make things happen. It's our fundamental nature and much of our behavior from infancy until the day we die. This is an expression of our need to exercise control over our environment and over our lives.

Implementation is simple but not easy. You need to commit yourself and consistently do the things that are necessary to ensure the healthy, happy growth of your children.

- Choose 3-4 goals of 11 which you believe are most important and most relevant for the growth of your children.
- Write a few sentences for each of the goal that you choose.
- How can you implement these values to life? How will you take action in the form of small, daily shifts.

The Sistine Chapel, the theory of relativity, the Eiffel Tower, racial equality, the moon-landing everything, every achievement was once a vivid mental image in the mind of its designer.

Dane Rudyard put it this way - ***"Man can only become what he's able to consciously imagine."***

About Author

Bhushan Khairnar

Bhushan Khairnar is Child Growth Consultant, Design Strategist, Investor and Life Mentor for more than decade. He has been engaged with startups and mature businesses and help them to transform the businesses to grow exponentially. He has founded Tesla Nests, Brunch Books, Dr. Kadaknath, Tolstoy World, Signdoks, Keyy and other 12 companies and helping bunch of other businesses to find solution through design thinking and business strategies. He has authored more than 12 books and mentored more than 5000 individuals on one to one basis.

The book is a result of his 15 years and 2 months research and daily journaling about his child Aditya for 7 years since his birth. He has studied Global Parenting culture and psychology of parenting in the changing world. He has interacted with thousands of parents on one to one basis. The first draft of the book was of 465 pages. It took another 6 months to make every sentence meaningful and authentic and make it 50 page book.

About Brunch Books

Brunch Books are focused reading books. Just like brunch, they are like heavy and healthy breakfast sufficient enough for the whole day work. Brunch Books are designed in a way that it gives certain advantage over traditional books:

- Every Brunch Books provide clarity and objective of reading in Concept section. The concept section is available for free on Brunch Books website. Read every book with clarity.
- Brunch Books are between 5 pages to 50 pages. Hence, consumes less time. Brunch Books are not summaries or abridged version of the book. The content are developed in a way that they provide you sufficient details and clarity in less pages without compromising with the flavour of reading.
- Every Brunch Book comes with Implementation Section. After reading the book, usually you need to find your way to implement the ideas your own ways. That's many time confusing and involves the task of taking notes and defining the correct way to implement the ideas that you learn from the book. Author himself/herself provide you with the clear guide to implement the ideas that has been presented by the author in the book.
- Every Brunch Book is written by the expert in specific area. After reading the book, readers usually are left with unanswered questions. With Brunch Books, you can email Author and get answer of your queries related to the book topic. Stay connected with the author.
- Brunch Books are focused on transforming you to the next level. We believe everyone reads with purpose. Reading is the best way of utilising time and energy. Hence, the books that are created to help you do better in your life are Brunch Books.
- Brunch Books can be written by anyone who have expertise in specified area. You don't need to be expert in language or expression in words. The clarity of format and the support by Brunch Book team, allows every expert to share his life long expertise and experience with the world. Every expert and experienced person now can write the Book. The traditional book formats did not allow to write book to the real experts who don't know how to write a book.

- Brunch Books is the World's First platform to provide Block-chain based registry to each book. They are stored in decentralised servers and secured by hash-codes.

Reference And Citations

- A Radical Awakening: Turn Pain into Power, Embrace Your Truth, Live Free by Dr Shefali Tsabary
- M, Furlong; S, McGilloway; T, Bywater; J, Hutchings; Sm, Smith; M, Donnelly (15 February 2012). "Behavioural and Cognitive-Behavioural Group-Based Parenting Programmes for Early-Onset Conduct Problems in Children Aged 3 to 12 Years". The Cochrane Database of Systematic Reviews (2): CD008225. doi:10.1002/14651858.CD008225.pub2. PMID 22336837.
- Sharenting & Oversharenting Archived 16 August 2016 at the Wayback Machine
- "WHAT WAS MY TEENAGER THINKING?". Talking to Teens. 26 September 2017. Retrieved 12 February 2018.
- “Lifebook" by Jon Butcher
- "7 Things Most Parents Get Wrong About Teen Drinking". Talking to Teens. 7 July 2017. Retrieved 12 February 2018.
- Jane B. Brooks (28 September 2012). The Process of Parenting: Ninth Edition. McGraw-Hill Higher Education. ISBN 978-0-07-746918-4. For the legal definition of parenting and parenthood see: Haim Abraham, A Family Is What You Make It? Legal Recognition and Regulation of Multiple Parents (2017)
- Bernstein, Robert (20 February 2008). "Majority of Children Live With Two Biological Parents". Archived from the original on 20 April 2008. Retrieved 26 March 2009.
- Johri, Ashish (2 March 2014). "6 Steps for Parents So Your Child is Successful". humanenrich.com. Retrieved 2 March 2014.
- Schechter, D.S., & Willheim, E. (2009). Disturbances of attachment and parental psychopathology in early childhood. Infant and Early Childhood Mental Health Issue. Child and Adolescent Psychiatry Clinics of North America, 18(3), 665-87.
- Grienenberger, J., Kelly, K. & Slade, A. (2005). Maternal Reflective Functioning, Mother-Infant Affective Communication and Infant Attachment: Exploring The Link Between Mental States and Observed Caregiving. Attachment and Human Development, 7, 299-311.
- Lieberman, A.F.; Padrón, E.; Van Horn, P.; Harris, W.W. (2005). "Angels

in the nursery: The intergenerational transmission of benevolent parental influences". Infant Ment. Health J. 26 (6): 504–20. CiteSeerX 10.1.1.964.1341. doi:10.1002/imhj.20071. PMID 28682485.

- Lareau, Annette (2002). "Invisible Inequality: Social Class and Child Rearing in Black Families and White Families". American Sociological Review. 67 (5): 747–76. doi:10.2307/3088916. JSTOR 3088916.
- shizuka, P. (2019). Social Class, Gender, and Contemporary Parenting Standards in the United States: Evidence from a National Survey Experiment. Social Forces, 98(1), 31–58. https://doi.org/10.1093/sf/soy107/ref>
- "20th Century Evolution of American Parenting Styles". Retrieved 11 May 2015..
- Weiten, W.; McCann, D. (2007). Themes and Variations. Nelson Education Ltd: Thomson Wadsworth. ISBN 978-0-17-647273-3.
- "Social class in parenting". Budingstar. 7 January 2020.
- Doob, Christopher (2013) (in English). Social Inequality and Social Stratification (1st ed. ed.). Boston: Pearson. p. 165.
- Baumrind, D. (1967). Child care practices anteceding three patterns of preschool behavior. Genetic Psychology Monographs, 75, 43–88.
- Baumrind, D. (1971). Current patterns of parental authority" Developmental Psychology 4 (1, Pt. 2), 1–103.
- Baumrind, D. (1978). "Parental disciplinary patterns and social competence in children". Youth & Society. 9 (3): 238–76. doi:10.1177/0044118X7800900302. S2CID 140984313.
- McKay M (2006). Parenting practices in emerging adulthood: Development of a new measure. Thesis, Brigham Young University. Retrieved 9 February 2016.
- Santrock, J.W. (2007). A topical approach to life-span development, third Ed. New York: McGraw-Hill.
- Rubin, Mark (2015). "Social Class Differences in Mental Health: Do Parenting Style and Friendship Play a Role?". Mark Rubin Social Psychology Research. Retrieved 29 August 2017.
- Rubin, M.; Kelly, B M. (2015). "A cross-sectional investigation of parenting style and friendship as mediators of the relation between social class and mental health in a university community". International Journal for Equity in Health. 14 (87): 1–11. doi:10.1186/s12939-015-0227-2. PMC 4595251. PMID 26438013.
- Hedstrom, Ellen (2016). Parenting Style as a Predictor of Internal and

External Behavioural Symptoms in Children : The Child's Perspective.

- Joseph M. V., John J. (2008). Global Academic Society Journal: Social Science Insight, Vol. 1, No. 5, pp. 16-25. ISSN 2029-0365 "Impact of Parenting Styles on Child Development".
- Friedson, Michael (1 January 2016). "Authoritarian parenting attitudes and social origin: The multigenerational relationship of socioeconomic position to childrearing values". Child Abuse & Neglect. 51: 263–275. doi:10.1016/j.chiabu.2015.10.001. ISSN 0145-2134. PMID 26585215.
- Famlii (2 February 2015). "Parenting Styles and Wealth: Concerted Cultivation by Annette Lareau". Famlii. Retrieved 15 April 2021.
- Zahedani ZZ, Rezaee R, Yazdani Z, Bagheri S, Nabeiei P. J Adv Med Educ Prof. 2016; 4:130–4 ZAHED ZAHEDANI Z; REZAEE R; YAZDANI Z; BAGHERI S; NABEIEI P (2016). "The Influence of Parenting Style on Academic Achievement and Career Path". Journal of Advances in Medical Education & Professionalism. 4 (3): 130–134. PMC 4927255. PMID 27382580.
- Lassonde, Stephen (2017). "Authority, disciplinary intimacy & parenting in middle-class America". European Journal of Developmental Psychology. 14 (6): 714–732. doi:10.1080/17405629.2017.1300577. S2CID 151783083.
- "permissive parenting". MSU.EDU.
- Finkelhor, D.; Ormrod, R.; Turner, H.; Holt, M. (November 2009). "Pathways to Poly-Victimization" (PDF). Child Maltreatment. 14 (4): 316–29. doi:10.1177/1077559509347012. PMID 19837972. S2CID 14676857.
- Bolin, Inge. Growing Up in a Culture of Respect: Child Rearing in Highland Peru. Austin: University of Texas Press, 2006. Project MUSE.[page needed]
- Olcer, Sevinc; Aytar, Abide Gungor (25 August 2014). "A Comparative Study into Social Skills of Five-six Year Old Children and Parental Behaviors". Procedia - Social and Behavioral Sciences. 141: 976–995. doi:10.1016/j.sbspro.2014.05.167.
- Chase-Lansdale, Cherlin & Kiernan, 1995; Hetherington, 1992; Zill, Morrison & Coiro, 1993; Bumpass, Sweet & Martin, 1990; Hetherington, Bridges & Insabella, 1998
- Sanders, Matthew R. (2008). "Triple P-Positive Parenting Program as a public health approach to strengthening parenting" (PDF). Journal of Family Psychology. 22 (4): 506–17. CiteSeerX 10.1.1.1012.8778.

doi:10.1037/0893-3200.22.3.506. PMID 18729665.

- Common Sense Parenting, Burke, 1997, p. 83
- Better Home Discipline, Cutts, 1952, p. 7
- Barlow, Jane; Smailagic, Nadja; Huband, Nick; Roloff, Verena; Bennett, Cathy (17 May 2014). "Group-based parent training programmes for improving parental psychosocial health". The Cochrane Database of Systematic Reviews (5): CD002020. doi:10.1002/14651858.CD002020.pub4. ISSN 1469-493X. PMID 24838729.
- Day, Nicholas (9 April 2013). "Give Your Baby a Machete". Slate. Retrieved 19 April 2013.
- Bolin, Inge (2006). Growing Up in a Culture of Respect: Child Rearing in Highland Peru. University of Texas Press. pp. 63–67. ISBN 978-0-292-71298-0.
- Robert K. Thomas. 1958. "Cherokee Values and World View" Unpublished MS, University of North Carolina Available at: http://works.bepress.com/robert_thomas/40
- Bolin, Inge. Growing Up in a Culture of Respect: Child Rearing in Highland Peru. Austin: University of Texas Press, 2006. Project MUSE. Web. 13 May. 2014. <http://muse.jhu.edu/>.[page needed]
- Doan, Stacey N. (May 2017). "Consequences of 'Tiger' Parenting: A Cross-Cultural Study of Maternal Psychological Control and Children's Cortisol Stress Response". Developmental Science. 20 (3): 10. doi:10.1111/desc.12404. hdl:2027.42/136743. PMID 27146549.
- Day, Nicholas (10 April 2013). "Parental ethnotheories and how parents in America differ from parents everywhere else". Slate. Retrieved 19 April 2013.[verification needed]
- Archibald, Jo-Ann, (2008). Indigenous Storywork: Educating The Heart, Mind, Body and Spirit. Vancouver, British Columbia: The University of British Columbia Press.[page needed]
- Delgado-Gaitan, Concha (1994). "Consejos: The Power of Cultural Narratives". Anthropology & Education Quarterly. 25 (3): 298–316. doi:10.1525/aeq.1994.25.3.04x0146p. JSTOR 3195848.
- Brown, P. (2002). Everyone has to lie in Tzeltal. (pp. 241–75) Lawrence Erlbaum Associates Publishers, Mahwah, NJ.
- Paradise, Ruth; Rogoff, Barbara. "Side by Side: Learning by Observing and Pitching In". Journal of the Society of Psychological Anthropology: 102–37.
- Gaskins, Suzanne; Paradise, Ruth (2010). "Learning Through

Observation in Daily Life". In Lancy, David; Bock, John; Gaskins, Suzanne (eds.). The Anthropology of Learning in Childhood. United Kingdom: AltaMira Press.

- Lee, Richard M.; Grotevant, Harold D.; Hellerstedt, Wendy L.; Gunnar, Megan R. (December 2006). "Cultural socialization in families with internationally adopted children". Journal of Family Psychology. 20 (4): 571–580. doi:10.1037/0893-3200.20.4.571. ISSN 1939-1293. PMC 2398726. PMID 17176191.
- McHale, Susan M.; Crouter, Ann C.; Kim, Ji-Yeon; Burton, Linda M.; Davis, Kelly D.; Dotterer, Aryn M.; Swanson, Dena P. (September 2006). "Mothers‘ and Fathers’ Racial Socialization in African American Families: Implications for Youth". Child Development. 77 (5): 1387–1402. doi:10.1111/j.1467-8624.2006.00942.x. hdl:2027.42/97223. ISSN 0009-3920. PMID 16999806.
- Huguley, James P.; Wang, Ming-Te; Vasquez, Ariana C.; Guo, Jiesi (May 2019). "Parental ethnic–racial socialization practices and the construction of children of color’s ethnic–racial identity: A research synthesis and meta-analysis" (PDF). Psychological Bulletin. 145 (5): 437–458. doi:10.1037/bul0000187. ISSN 1939-1455. PMID 30896188. S2CID 84845230.
- Priest, Naomi; Walton, Jessica; White, Fiona; Kowal, Emma; Baker, Alison; Paradies, Yin (November 2014). "Understanding the complexities of ethnic-racial socialization processes for both minority and majority groups: A 30-year systematic review". International Journal of Intercultural Relations. 43: 139–155. doi:10.1016/j.ijintrel.2014.08.003. ISSN 0147-1767.
- Sedgh, Gilda; Singh, Susheela; Hussain, Rubina (10 September 2014). "Intended and Unintended Pregnancies Worldwide in 2012 and Recent Trends". Studies in Family Planning. 45 (3): 301–14. doi:10.1111/j.1728-4465.2014.00393.x. ISSN 0039-3665. PMC 4727534. PMID 25207494.
- Morris Eaves; Robert N. Essick; Joseph Viscomi (eds.). "Songs of Innocence and of Experience, copy AA, object 25 (Bentley 25, Erdman 25, Keynes 25) "Infant Joy"". William Blake Archive. Retrieved 16 January 2014.
- Gartner LM; Morton J; Lawrence RA; Naylor AJ; O'Hare D; Schanler RJ; Eidelman AI; et al. (February 2005). "Breastfeeding and the Use of Human Milk". Pediatrics. 115 (2): 496–506. doi:10.1542/

peds.2004-2491. PMID 15687461.
- van der Voort, Anja; Juffer, Femmie; J. Bakermans-Kranenburg, Marian (1 January 2014). Barlow, Jane (ed.). "Sensitive parenting is the foundation for secure attachment relationships and positive social-emotional development of children". Journal of Children's Services. 9 (2): 165–176. doi:10.1108/JCS-12-2013-0038. ISSN 1746-6660.
- SS, Hamilton. "Result Filters." National Center for Biotechnology Information. U.S. National Library of Medicine, 1 October 2008. Web. 13 March 2013.
- "Teaching Kids to Mind Their Manners: How to Raise a Polite Child".
- "The Terrible Twos Explained – Safe Kids (UK)". Safe Kids. 10 May 2011. Retrieved 2 May 2012.
- Pitman, Teresa. "Toddler Frustration". Todaysparent. Retrieved 3 December 2011.
- Schechter, Daniel S.; Willheim, Erica; Hinojosa, Claudia; Scholfield-Kleinman, Kimberly; Turner, J. Blake; McCaw, Jaime; Zeanah, Charles H.; Myers, Michael M. (2010). "Subjective and Objective Measures of Parent-Child Relationship Dysfunction, Child Separation Distress, and Joint Attention". Psychiatry. 73 (2): 130–44. doi:10.1521/psyc.2010.73.2.130. PMID 20557225. S2CID 5132495.
- Schechter, Daniel S.; Zygmunt, Annette; Coates, Susan W.; Davies, Mark; Trabka, Kimberly A.; McCaw, Jaime; Kolodji, Ann; Robinson, Joann L. (2007). "Caregiver traumatization adversely impacts young children's mental representations on the MacArthur Story Stem Battery". Attachment & Human Development. 9 (3): 187–205. doi:10.1080/14616730701453762. PMC 2078523. PMID 18007959.
- Levendosky, Alytia A.; Leahy, Kerry L.; Bogat, G. Anne; Davidson, William S.; von Eye, Alexander (2006). "Domestic violence, maternal parenting, maternal mental health, and infant externalizing behavior". Journal of Family Psychology. 20 (4): 544–52. doi:10.1037/0893-3200.20.4.544. PMID 17176188.
- "American Time Use Survey". Bureau of Labor Statistics. 24 June 2015.
- Kenneth R. Ginsburg. "The Importance of Play in Promoting Healthy Child Development and Maintaining Strong Parent-Child Bonds" (PDF). American Academy of Pediatrics. Archived from the original (PDF) on 11 October 2009.
- Hoskins, Donna (18 September 2014). "Consequences of Parenting on Adolescent Outcomes". Societies. 4 (3): 506–531. doi:10.3390/

soc4030506. ISSN 2075-4698.

- Newman, Kathy; Harrison, Lynda; Dashiff, Carol; Davies, Susan (February 2008). "Relationships between parenting styles and risk behaviors in adolescent health: an integrative literature review". Revista Latino-Americana de Enfermagem. 16 (1): 142–150. doi:10.1590/S0104-11692008000100022. ISSN 0104-1169. PMID 18392544.
- Mikko Myrskylä; Rachel Margolis (2014). "Happiness: Before and After the Kids". Demography. 51 (5): 1843–66. CiteSeerX 10.1.1.454.2051. doi:10.1007/s13524-014-0321-x. PMID 25143019. S2CID 8127506.
- https://www.nordangliaeducation.com/
- https://mamadisrupt.com/
- https://www.ncbi.nlm.nih.gov/
- https://www.unlockfood.ca/
- https://www.davuniversity.org/

Printed by Libri Plureos GmbH in Hamburg,
Germany